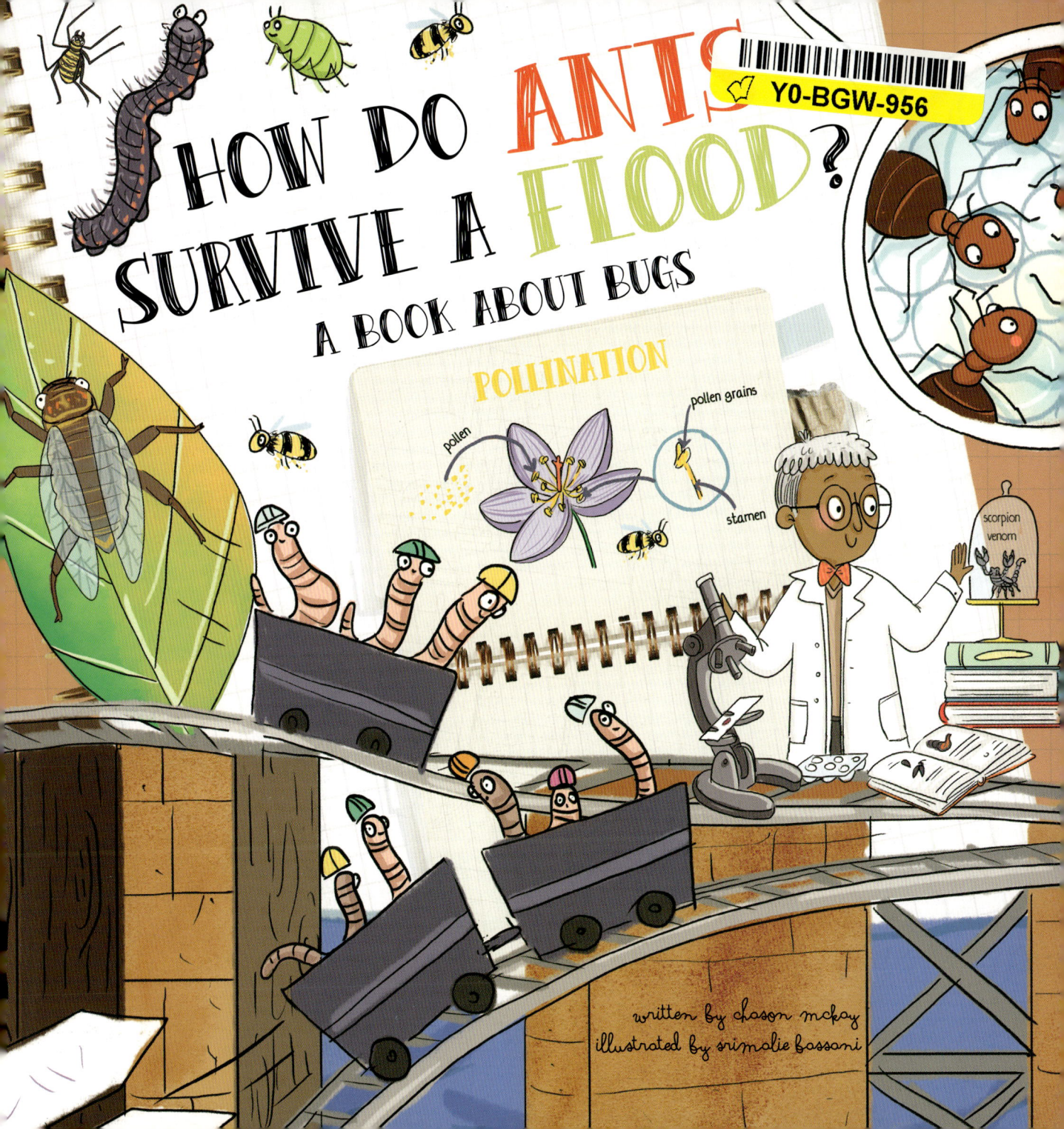

Bugs are INCREDIBLE!

Next time you think about squishing a spider or squashing an ant...don't! Why?

Because bugs are amazing! They live incredible lives and have countless talents and abilities. They can glow and dance and dazzle and sing. Our lives wouldn't be the same without bugs because they help us in so many ways.

Did you know bugs are over 400 million years old? That's older than dinosaurs! Not to mention bugs make up more than half of all living things on Earth. The reason bugs are so old and scattered across the planet is because they are great at adapting to their environments. It doesn't matter if it's as hot as the desert or as cold as your freezer, bugs can find a way to make just about anywhere their home.

Scorpion venom isn't always bad. Scientists actually use scorpion venom to treat arthritis and other diseases.

Cockroaches can live for a week without water. If that's not impressive enough, they can go a whole MONTH without food!

How do ants survive a flood? Do they ready a ship and call up their captain?

No, they don't have a real ship. But they do have a raft...sort of.

When it starts to flood, ants form a living raft by holding on tightly to each other. Tiny hairs on the ants trap enough air underneath the raft to keep it afloat. It takes two minutes for the ants to create their raft, and they can live connected together like this for several weeks.

Ants know it's time to form a raft by passing notes to each other in the form of chemicals they release called pheromones. Ants read the pheromones by using their two antennae located on top of their heads.

As earthworms burrow through the ground, they help turn soil into food for plants to eat and allow space for water and nutrients to reach the soil.

When bees buzz around flowers to collect nectar, some of the pollen from the flowers sticks to the tiny hairs on the bee's body. When the bee flies to the next flower, some of the pollen rubs off of the bee and onto the new flower, which then pollinates the plant. The bees then use the pollen and nectar they have collected from the flowers of plants to make honey.

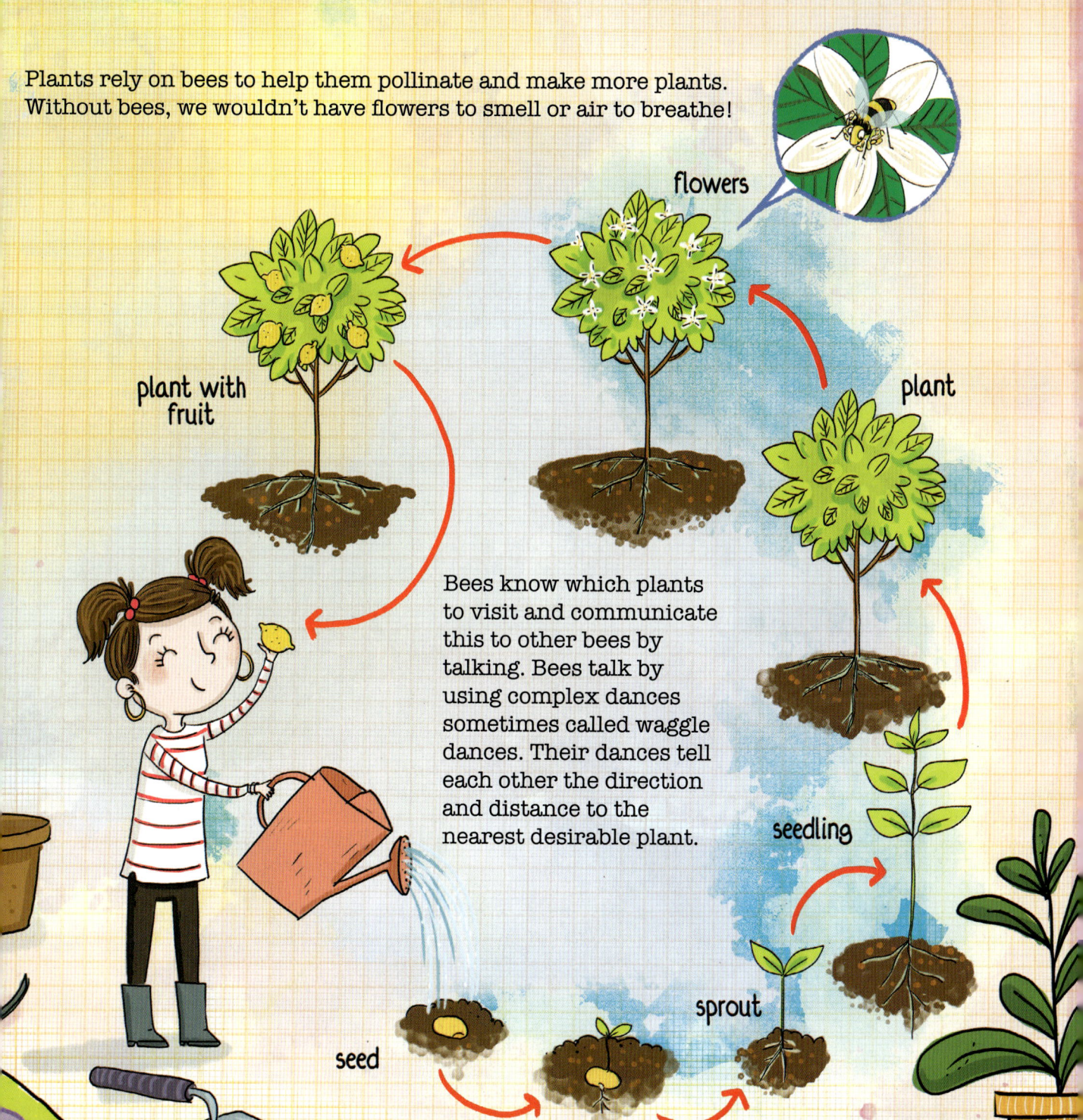

How do ladybugs help farmers protect their crops? Do they dress up as monsters to scare off pests?

No, but that would be funny.

Instead, adult ladybugs eat plant-eating insects like aphids and mealybugs which are known for destroying crops. Not only do ladybugs help by eating the mealybugs and aphids, adult ladybugs lay hundreds of eggs in groups of these plant-eating pests so that the baby ladybugs can help protect future crops too.

Ladybugs have even done their job in space! In 1999, NASA astronaut Eileen Collins led a mission to space and brought aphids and four ladybugs with her to study how the bugs would interact in a zero-gravity environment. On Earth, aphids can escape from ladybugs by falling off of leaves. However, in space, falling is impossible without gravity, meaning the aphids were in serious trouble.

How do cicadas sing songs? Do they play guitar and belt out tunes around a campfire?

No, cicadas do like to sing during summer nights, but their songs can actually be louder than rock and roll shows!

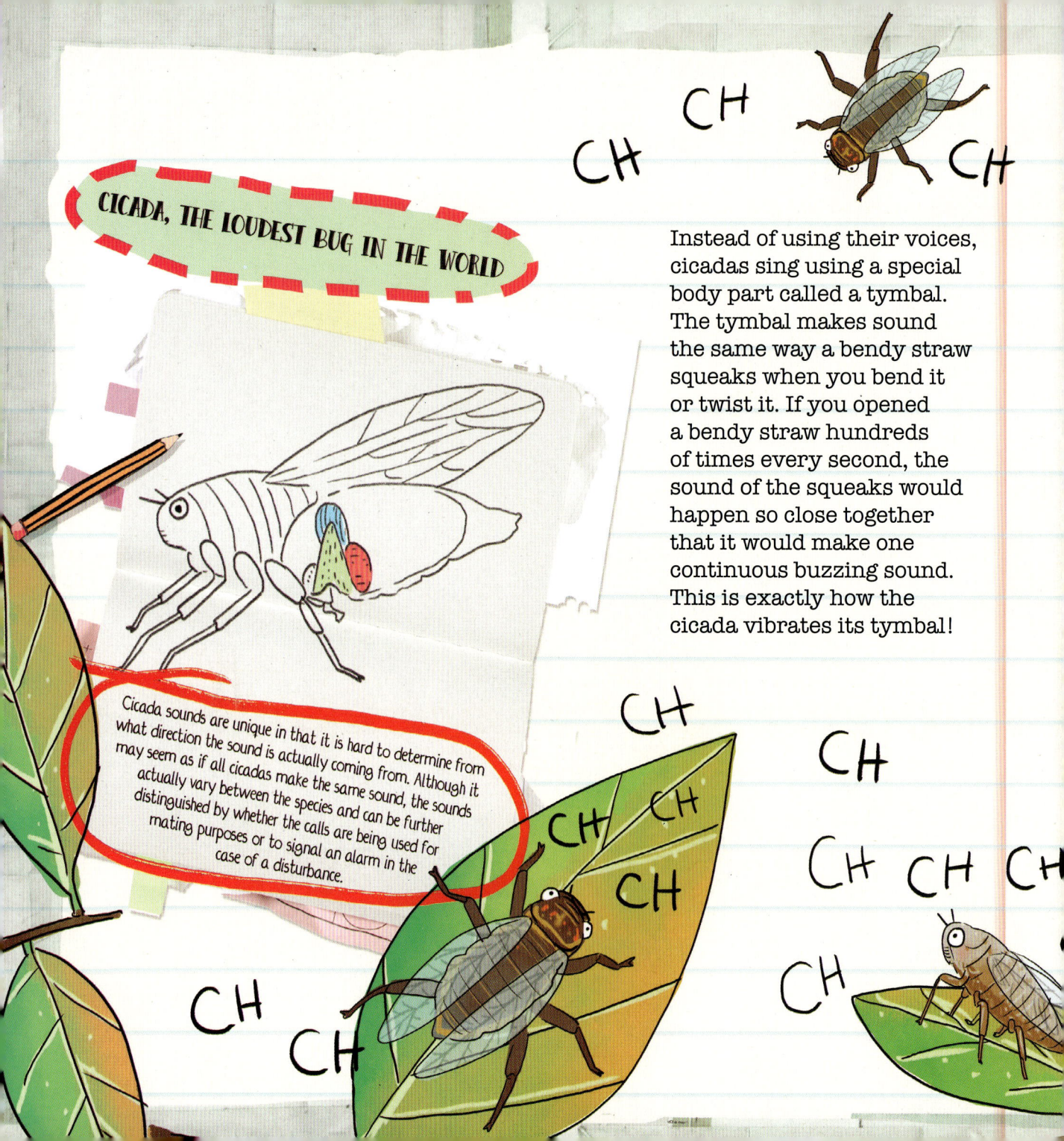

CICADA, THE LOUDEST BUG IN THE WORLD

Instead of using their voices, cicadas sing using a special body part called a tymbal. The tymbal makes sound the same way a bendy straw squeaks when you bend it or twist it. If you opened a bendy straw hundreds of times every second, the sound of the squeaks would happen so close together that it would make one continuous buzzing sound. This is exactly how the cicada vibrates its tymbal!

Cicada sounds are unique in that it is hard to determine from what direction the sound is actually coming from. Although it may seem as if all cicadas make the same sound, the sounds actually vary between the species and can be further distinguished by whether the calls are being used for mating purposes or to signal an alarm in the case of a disturbance.

Cicadas can be heard from over a mile and a half (2.4 kilometers) away, and the loudest cicadas can make sounds as loud as 120 decibels. That's as loud as a thunderclap!

fireworks, ambulances	140 db	Painful & Dangerous
	130 db	
jet planes, cicadas	120 db	Uncomfortable
hair dryers, snowmobiles, sporting events, blenders	110 db / 100 db / 90 db	Very Loud
alarm clocks, traffic, vacuum	80 db / 70 db	Loud
refrigerator, normal conversation	60 db / 50 db	Moderate
whispering, quiet library	40 db / 30 db	Soft
leaves rustling	20 db / 10 db	Faint
	0 db	

Do you think these earplugs will help with the cicada sound?

A sound level meter is used for acoustic measurements. Acoustics is the science of studying sound as it travels through solids, liquids, and gases. This differs from electrical audio, audio that travels electronically through cables and audio components.

Like bats and owls, spiders also like to sleep during the day and come out at night. Because spiders sometimes go months without eating, they have learned how to pass the time by hibernating or sleeping for long periods of time. When a spider hibernates, it slows down its heart rate and stays totally still to save energy.

1. Go outside and collect natural materials (leaves, pine cones, tree bark, wood chips, nut shells, etc.) and pack them inside your empty cardboard box which will be your bug hotel.
2. Check your recycling for some recyclables (toilet paper roll, scrap paper, cardboard, milk cartons, ice pop sticks, etc.). Bottles and small boxes are great for packing bug hotels.
3. Once you've packed your bug hotel, find a spot outside to place your masterpiece and wait for some bug friends to move in.

PAPER PLATE BUGS

Turn a paper plate into a ladybug, spider, or any other bug you like!

Here's what you'll need: glue, pipe cleaners, googly eyes, construction paper, safety scissors, and paper plates

1. To make a spider, start by painting the bottom side of a paper plate black. Set aside to let the paint dry.

2. Using safety scissors, cut an oval out of black construction paper. This is what will be used to make the spider's head.

3. Pick out 4 googly eyes and glue them to the oval to give your spider eyes.

4. Once the painted plate is dry, glue the spider's head to the bottom of the plate. Then poke 4 holes down the left side of the plate and 4 holes down the right side of the plate.

5. Thread a pipe cleaner through the first 2 holes, bending both ends.

6. Repeat 3 more times until your spider has all 8 legs!

Glue the head to the bottom side of the plate like this.

spider

1. To make a ladybug, start by painting the bottom side of a paper plate red. Set aside to let the paint dry.

2. Using safety scissors, cut an oval or semi-circle out of black construction paper to use for the ladybug's head. Cut 6 small circles out of black construction paper to use for the ladybug's spots. Then cut out a long, thin triangle that is the same length as the plate.

3. Once the paper plate is dry, glue the black triangle in the middle of the plate to create the wings. Then glue the black oval to the top of the triangle as the head. Finally glue 3 black spots on each side of the red plate.

4. Glue 2 googly eyes on the black oval to give your ladybug eyes.

5. Once the glue is dry, poke two small holes in the head and thread a pipe cleaner through both of the holes to make the antennae.

6. Poke 3 small holes on the left side and 3 small holes on the right side of your ladybug and thread a pipe cleaner through each hole. Twist the ends of each pipe cleaner around to give your ladybug 6 legs.

ladybug

bee

Glue head here

Triangle goes here

Try making a bee!

GLOSSARY

Antennae – thin, moveable body parts on insects' heads that are used to feel the surrounding environment

Aphids – very small insects that live in large colonies and feed by sucking the juices from plants

Arachnid – a category of animals; arachnids have eight legs, no antennae, and bodies divided into two sections; spiders, scorpions, and ticks are arachnids

Castings – fertilizer that is created from the excrement of a worm that has digested organic matter

Decibel – a unit used to measure the intensity of sound; some cicadas can produce sounds up to 120 decibels

Hibernate – an insect's period of inactivity that is caused by low temperatures

Ladybug Life Cycle – ladybugs' lifetimes are divided into four stages: egg stage, larval stage, pupa stage, and adult stage

Mealybugs – small insects that have a white, waxy covering and are known for their destruction of crops

Organic Matter – material that comes from the decay of an organism that has recently died

Pheromones – chemicals produced by insects that are used to attract other insects of the same type

Pollen – powder produced by a flower's male parts and used to fertilize the flower's female parts

Pollination – the process by which insects transport pollen from a flower's male parts to its female parts

Setae – hair-like structures on insects that can be used to aid movement or as a defense mechanism

Stigma – a flower structure that is part of the plant's female organs and is used to trap pollen

Tymbal – a cicada's body part that is used to produce sound

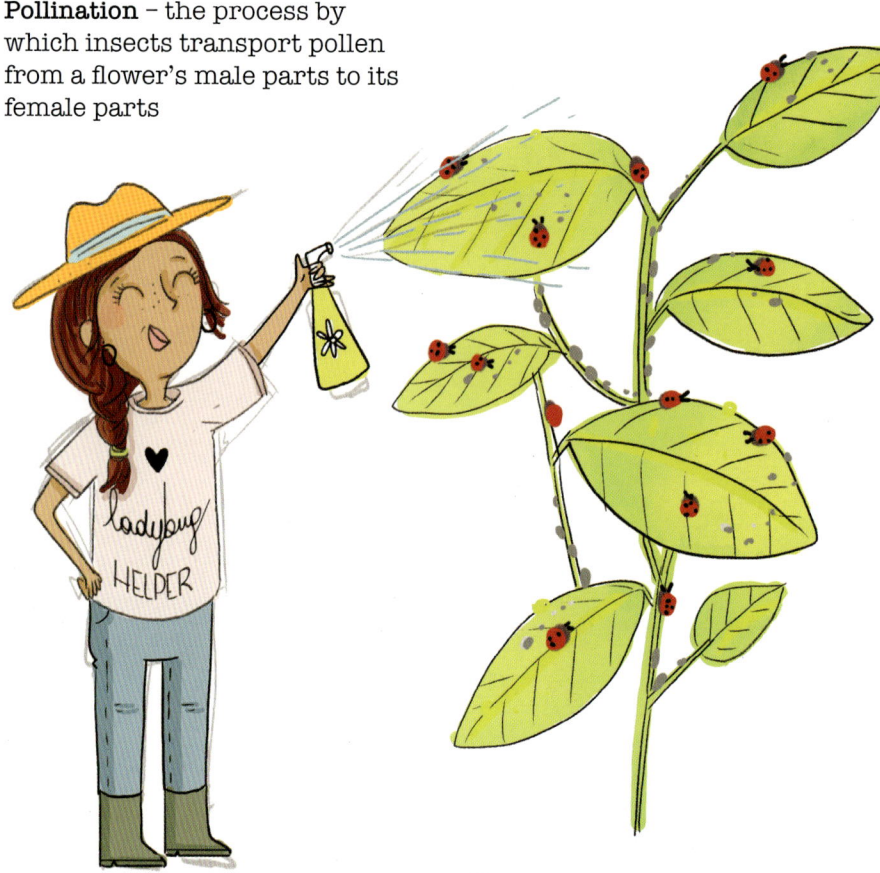